THE HISTORICAL STUDY OF
ANGLO-AMERICAN DEMOCRACY

T0345978

THE
HISTORICAL STUDY OF
ANGLO-AMERICAN
DEMOCRACY

An Inaugural Lecture

BY

ROY F. NICHOLS

Visiting Professor of American History and Institutions
in the University of Cambridge

CAMBRIDGE
AT THE UNIVERSITY PRESS
1949

CAMBRIDGE
UNIVERSITY PRESS

University Printing House, Cambridge CB2 8BS, United Kingdom

Cambridge University Press is part of the University of Cambridge.

It furthers the University's mission by disseminating knowledge in the pursuit of education, learning and research at the highest international levels of excellence.

www.cambridge.org
Information on this title: www.cambridge.org/9781107494664

© Cambridge University Press 1949

First published 1949
Re-issued 2015

A catalogue record for this publication is available from the British Library

ISBN 978-1-107-49466-4 Paperback

THE HISTORICAL STUDY OF
ANGLO-AMERICAN DEMOCRACY

I. *An Experiment in Anglo-American*
Scholarly Co-operation

An American historian passing through the Great Gate
of Trinity, or walking in the courts of Emmanuel, is at
once reminded of the cultural kinship of Great Britain
and the United States. These Cambridge surroundings
recall to him the fact that the University was the
birthplace of much of significance in American culture.
In the days of colonial beginnings, an unusually large
number of English University men came to New
England. Massachusetts was scarce six years old
when in this wilderness the founders must create a new
Cambridge with as much of the academic ritual as they
could muster. On the first board of overseers of this
wilderness cloister were five Trinity men and one from
Emmanuel. The new Cambridge was called Harvard,
after John Harvard of Emmanuel. The first governor
of the colony was John Winthrop of Trinity, and of
the 134 University men in New England in these
early years one-quarter were from Emmanuel. These

Cambridge men laid carefully the firm foundation for a strong edifice, a foundation that has ever supported effectively the increasingly complex superstructure.

The creation of the Professorship in American History and Institutions in such a favourable environment has presented to the world of scholarship new opportunities for significant contributions. My esteemed predecessors in this chair have made clear some of these possibilities, and I can but carry on from where they left off. To my mind the nature of this opportunity may be described somewhat as follows.

The close familial tie which binds Britons and Americans has produced an interesting institutional relationship. But it is a relationship somewhat difficult to understand. Many institutions and culture patterns exist in both societies bearing the same names and too easily inviting the careless assumption that they are the same thing. This is not necessarily accurate, for it is a fact that institutions bearing the same designation may be quite different even in related societies.

The English language is not always an esperanto for Anglo-Americans; in fact, the common rumour that those in the United Kingdom and those in the United States speak the same tongue can be a hindrance to understanding. The unwarranted confidence that there is unilingual communication across the water gives rise to the careless assumption that there is no problem of comprehension. Often, therefore, there is no effort at avoiding misunderstanding because complete understanding is assumed. A little more care would often make for a more profitable meeting of minds.

In better developing interoceanic interchange it is necessary to realize that institutions that leave a mature culture, a metropolis, and migrate across the sea to become established on a far-off frontier suffer more than a sea-change. They leave an atmosphere of care and calculation, of thrift and relative scarcity, and are re-established in a stimulating environment marked by an abundance of resources and an encouraging exuberance of spirit and optimism which become congenital. In the younger newer culture these institutions retain the same names but they may not be really too similar. The association of scholars of two cultures such as the creation of this chair provides, makes possible co-operative studies of problems of this type. And the solution of some of them can contribute much to the world's understanding of intercultural relationship.

II. *American Patterns of Historical Scholarship*

Before discussing possible methods of intellectual co-operation it is well for us to consider briefly the background of American historians so that those in England may compare it with their own immediate antecedents and their own criteria of thought. Such a discussion will make plainer the possibility of co-operation. The succession of scholars who come to sojourn with you, to exchange ideas with you and perhaps to join with you in opening new paths, come from an experience in historical working and thinking which will give its colouring to whatever they may undertake in Cambridge.

We, who come from the University world of the United States as students of history, appear in your midst fresh from discussions arising from a new effort to give more valid meaning to history. In recent years we have been giving much attention to that subjective starting-point of the historian's thinking, so long ignored or ignorantly denied, namely, the 'frame of reference' of the individual historian. There has been a vigorous contest over subjectivity and objectivity which has opened closets, revealed skeletons and all told stirred up much heartening intellectual activity. Being one who has discovered what he thinks is his frame of reference, it is only fair that I give you the opportunity to read the label on this scholar's gown.

Just about the time that the noted historian who once cultivated his genius at Trinity, Lord Macaulay, began the publication of his great history—and the year just passed was the year of its centenary—the first of the famed American historians, George Bancroft, was giving his thoughts to his fellow-countrymen and to the world. He presented the first real achievement in American historiography, and his work was marked by significant characteristics. He made extensive research in original sources, he had literary competence and he developed an interpretation, he attempted to give meaning to the American experience. To him the American Republic was a great climax in the work of Divine Providence. In developing this interpretation he but reflected the spirit of mission which was so strong among his fellow-Americans in those days. This was but another way of proclaiming liberty to the monarchical and aristocratic polities of Europe. It was a somewhat flamboyant manifestation of the passion for nationalism which was a phase of the Romantic Movement of the early nineteenth century. This tradition became firmly established among American historians and can be easily discovered. It resembles the Whig tradition that Macaulay so exalted in British historiography.

Under this influence much of our political and therefore our schoolbook history has continued. Hardly had Bancroft and his disciples, later aided by some remarks from abroad such as Gladstone made about the Constitution, started well on their work of establishing a hagiology among our colonial and revolutionary ancestors, when the lamentable Civil War almost sundered the Republic. The triumph of the Union forces, the tragic death of the martyred Lincoln, and the speed with which certain political and military leaders broke into print, produced a renewed outburst of nationalistic patriotism and a decidedly liberal interpretation. The war had been a triumph of the forces of right and liberty, resulting in the strengthening of the republican form of government and the freeing of the slave. It was a triumph of liberalism.

In the midst of this demonstration of the strength and righteousness of democracy the industrial revolution, operating in a region so rich in natural resources and so well supplied with capital and labour, began to bear fruit. Great corporations and fabulously wealthy entrepreneurs began to rise meteorically on the American business sky. The power which these corporations and individuals amassed was used in part to make their own share of the results of their operation much the larger. Poverty, oppression and various legal or almost legal forms of larceny, plus the unhappy results of the operation of certain natural forces, meant that too large a proportion of the population, whether labouring directly in industry or not, had to pay tribute to these controllers of the national wealth. Political protest was organized under the banners of domestic party organizations whose leaders demanded that the government exercise powers of control which would protect the rights and the standard of living of the people at large.

Dynamic figures like William J. Bryan, Theodore Roosevelt, Woodrow Wilson, Robert M. La Follette and Franklin Delano Roosevelt, all of them eloquent in expressing the prevailing political thought of the nation, elaborated the ideas of Jefferson, Webster and Lincoln and produced an interpretation of our history which became current just as a spate of school texts was being written in response to a growing demand for history teaching in the schools.

The result of this has been that, as in England there is the definite Whig tradition dominating historical thinking, which Butterfield describes, there is in the United States a dominant Democratic or Progressive tradition. This stems from the American Revolution

11

and Bancroft just as the English Whig tradition grew from the Puritan Revolution and Macaulay.

Within fifty years after Macaulay and Bancroft a second and sometimes conflicting tendency developed in American historical writing. This reflected European practice likewise. Many of the American students who went to the German Universities for postgraduate study during the latter half of the nineteenth century sat in the lecture rooms and seminars of the new 'scientific' school of German historians.

They came home to think of history not so much as literature, not so much as the stirring story of a wonder-working Providence, but as science. They were to seek and clarify data and then formulate law such as the natural sciences could compass. The chief impression that these German savants made upon their American disciples was twofold. There was to be method and objectivity. Elaborate concepts of method and criticism were built up. 'Lehrbücher' were written and the seminar was recognized, as its name implied, as the seed bed in which would be cultivated the young plants of this scientific history. These students came back to the United States, and through their efforts graduate study was organized in the new university atmosphere which began to develop about 1890.

The new generation of professors of history was intensely interested in method, and their instruction was frequently almost exclusively confined to the multifarious directions in Bernheim and Langlois and Seignobos. These disciples of scientific history were dedicated to the great principle of objectivity which, together with the method, would reveal everything 'wie es eigentlich gewesen war'. Truth came that way. As I understand it the English Universities were never so overwhelmingly impressed. While due respect was paid to objectivity, and Professor Bury dedicated history at Cambridge to the status of science, nevertheless, English historians avoided the confining bounds of the seminar and methodological overweight.

The result of this scientific preoccupation in America was a much more critical attitude toward sources, a keen interest in a genetic theory of institutional development and a liberal use of the comparative method of seeking similar institutions in different societies. The main interest was political, and many could agree with Freeman that history was past politics. The politics and the political institutions quite frequently emerged from the German forests and reached America via the British Isles. The emphasis on objectivity, however, developed a tendency to let the facts tell the story. The historian, by applying his critical methods, had come to believe that he could discover the facts and that their arrangement in proper sequence, generally chronological, would give the result needed without the intervention of the historian's original thinking or the employment of much if any subjective element. Much of this work, particularly in the form of doctoral dissertations, was heavy, compendious and without meaning.

The questions of meaning took on more and more importance as the years of the twentieth century began to take shape. Frederick Jackson Turner rebelled against the genetic theory, that previous European experience was the dominant influence in shaping American institutions, and developed a hypothesis of environmental determinism which he preached with a romantic nationalistic fervour. Charles Austin Beard, fresh from Oxford and the Ruskin school, examined the basis of constitutional structure and produced 'an economic interpretation' of the Constitution.

Almost simultaneously there occurred a revolt against the exclusive sway of political history. History to have meaning must be conceived of as more than past politics. The field was much more complex than hitherto considered, and the scope of research must be widened. Beard's interest in economic factors reflected a growing preoccupation in economic history such as was evidenced in Cambridge by Cunningham.

These tendencies were interrupted by World War I, and at the close of that conflict a new flood of influences broke over dykes and complicated the struggle for meaning. The unlocking of the archives by Russia and Germany, the controversy over war guilt, produced new interest in sources and the interpretation of diplomatic action. Much work in the history of international relations was done by Gooch and Temperley and continues to be done by Butler. In America a new school of diplomatic history was raised to which one of my predecessors, Perkins, has made significant contribution.

A second post-war tendency was a further demand that history should plumb greater depths. In academic circles there was a greater sense of history as the story of the life of the people. Green in England and McMaster in the United States had written histories of the people of their respective countries, and there now developed an interest in social history. A co-operative series, the *History of American Life*, was brought to a successful conclusion. At the same time, through the instrumentality of the newly organized Social Science Research Council and a tendency toward closer association in the Universities, historians, economists, sociologists, political scientists, anthropologists and psychologists were brought into more frequent contact. One of the results of this contact was that historians, to some extent, gained a more accurate concept of society and its significant behaviour patterns, and began to include within their research interests the tracing of the evolution of these patterns, in ways described by Postan. This was accomplished in part by a shift from national to local history. A regional school developed which studied the sections of the United States as entities. Their cultures and social habits were subjects of intensive study. Another of my predecessors, Dobie, represented this trend particularly in relation to the study of folklore.

At the same time a literary revolt was staged. The 'scientific' tendencies had served to make history heavy; ponderous analyses of evidence and much citation of authority had cluttered the pages. Furthermore, literary skill was suspect as evidence of distaste for the necessary scientific analysis and weighing of evidence, and 'fine writing' was sneered at. But the tradition of Bancroft, Parkman, Prescott and Motley was attractive and invited a renaissance. It came particularly in the form of biography, and efforts were made to restore to historians a sense of literary responsibility. This is so effectively represented at

Cambridge by the Master of Trinity. My immediate predecessor, Commager, has laboured effectively in this vineyard.

Closely allied with this came the interest in the culture, the creative power, the thought behind the action. The real source of history was the working of the minds of men, and its object should be the study of the history of ideas, the development of attitudes, the history of the traditions of the people. This has produced an interest in intellectual history which has been one of the most significant achievements of this troubled century.

The vision of this wider horizon has certainly stimulated a correspondingly greater variety of research and writing. It has likewise encouraged a tendency to specialization, to fragmentation, and has produced a passion for labelling amounting to an adjectival war. Specialists flourish by adjectival designation. Scholars are known as political, economic, social, cultural, diplomatic, or intellectual historians. The situation is as bad as in the medical profession, where an eye and ear man will not venture down one's throat and refuses to indulge in any fancies regarding one's digestion or even respiration.

To a certain extent these tendencies brought new meaning to the fruits of the American historian's labour, but they also brought confusion approaching chaos. With this plethora of adjectives, this intensity of specialization, what had become of history and its meaning? American historians had taken up this question with more or less earnestness when Henry Adams began to circulate his speculations on the meaning of history among his professional associates. He and his brother Brooks had been considering various possible interpretations, and Henry seemed most impressed by certain discoveries in physics, notably the second law of thermodynamics which described the dissipation of energy. Adams propounded the possibility that there might be a law dictating the dissipation of intellectual energy, and that man might be witnessing the running down of his mental creative capacity.

While this pessimistic view of things, buttressed somewhat by Spengler and world events, had its influence in promoting a certain degree of discouragement, the prevailing optimism rather brushed it aside. However, this interest of Adams did stimulate a greater concern to study the findings of science, to discover analogies. Physics, meteorology and biology yielded some which provoked discussion.

The greatest influence of this type of thinking by scientific analogies came between the wars, when the findings of the twentieth-century physicists began to be sensed by the laity. Such concepts as relativity, indeterminancy, and the unmaterial basis of matter made the historian further doubt the possibility of objectivity and the discovery of the whole truth about the past. Historians took refuge in a new concept. Historical truth was not to be absolute but relative. Objectivity was not possible in the absolute sense. Everything depended actually upon the historian, upon his training, his frame of reference, his health, himself. Strive as the historian might his objectivity would be bound by the subjective; the truth which he could discover would be only relative. So he must be content with objective relativity and strive to discover first of all what influences were shaping his frame of reference and then proceed to be as objective as he could. The realization of this concept seemed to some to invite a form of nihilism—the truth in history was unobtainable—the historian's effort was vain.

Others disdained this sense of futility. They maintained that if the historian did not claim too much, if he were careful to ask the right questions, those which his data and his technique would permit him to answer, he could slowly and painstakingly advance the limits of certainty. These qualifications were chastening but they dispelled nihilism.

A third group was mindful of another, shall we say, more philosophical influence. At the same time that discussion finally developed in the United States regarding Henry Adams's concern over dissipation of intellectual energy, the work of Benedetto Croce arrived in the form of a much-debated translation. 'History is the eternal spirit, individualizing itself. The spirit itself is history, the maker of history. History is thought. This spirit becomes transparent to itself as thought in the consciousness of the historian.' Croce-ism was revived when Collingwood's posthumous *Idea of History*, including his analysis of Oakeshott, arrived in America. Certain among the historical guild saw history in another guise. The historian was the one who alone could rethink past thoughts and thus transmit past into present experience. Thus would history have real meaning. And at this point we now stand in America. Such American historians as visit you will be thinking along certain of these lines and bear one or the other of these labels. You will understand them better if you consider the categories into which they are divided.

III. Opportunity for Anglo-American Historical Co-operation

Having thus briefly outlined the background of American historiography and explained the varying points of view of American historians, I now turn to the main theme of this discussion, namely, the possibilities of intellectual co-operation between British and American historians. Let us canvass some of the opportunities offered by the new association.

The study of American history is not something which should be merely of peripheral interest in Britain. It is so closely related to so much of British history that the comparing of notes and exchanging of ideas should produce rich harvest. There is need for more history of the behaviour patterns and attitudes characteristic of the Anglo-American experience, a field which should transcend the barriers of nationalistic history.

Among the many problems in the development of this Atlantic civilization is the nature of the evolution of what we call 'democracy'. This term 'democracy' is not used in its narrow political sense but in its broader cultural definition. The developments on both sides of the Atlantic have borne an interesting relationship, embracing the story of the peculiar kinship of a parent society with mature culture, and a callow and obstreperous offspring in the difficult process of growing to maturity. The problem involves an understanding not only of the interaction of these cultures but also of the individual development of each, and it presents no mean exercise in synthesis, a challenge which should attract scholars on both sides of the water. For does it not seem obvious in these troubled times of ideological warfare in which we live that the two greatest of the democracies should make every effort to comprehend the meaning of the term? So much of any such comprehension depends upon accurate history.

The development of democracy in both Britain and the United States is, I believe, the most significant central theme for the history of these societies. The more we grasp the complications of our prevailing behaviour patterns and attitudes, and the history of our thought, the more we may validly maintain that the evolution of democracy has been the dominant force in Anglo-American cultural development.

Certainly in the United States and, if I read rightly, in Great Britain likewise, popular interest has been focused predominantly on political concepts. The Anglo-American people have thought in terms of rights, of liberty and of self-government. That in which they have taken greatest pride has been the achievement of their respective types of democracy. The development of this thought about, practice in and pride regarding self-government may well be a central theme which will be useful in considering the history of the United States and interpreting it in Great Britain. To-day in this war of ideologies we are eager enough to make democracy the distinguishing hall-mark of our joint declarations.

American and British scholars have their first common problems in interpreting conditions in the England of the late sixteenth and early seventeenth centuries. We should know much more than we do, in America at least, of the personal and institutional experience in England of those who ventured across the seas. We probably know more of their business and religious background than we do of their political experience. What was their political behaviour in England? What practice had they in elections, in administration?

The colonial experience itself invites further suggestion and study in England within the realm of colonial administration, a theme which should be of great interest to the students of the empire. In the United States we have viewed this development usually with the idea of accounting for the growth of the spirit of independence and less from the standpoint of non-nationalistic students of the problems of migration and imperial administration. How do students of empire here look upon the administrative methods developed, the civil servants dispatched? What were British attitudes toward the colonies? What were the colonists who wrote home saying, and how did their relatives and friends react? How did the colonies figure in the English literature of these times?

When we come to the parting of the ways in the years between 1763 and 1783 the secret is to be found in the subtleties of family relationship. Had the colonists not been so British the conflict might well not have occurred, certainly it would have taken a different course. The seventeenth-century British experience had produced everything necessary in the way of ideas and propaganda material. The colonists had only to read the exploits of their ancestors to find blue-prints for their own guidance. The American Revolution is but part and parcel of the same stream of behaviour which may be described as the history of the Anglo-American pattern of self-government.

After 1781, the study of the process of organizing the American Republic calls for more knowledge of British governmental practice, for the constitution makers in Philadelphia owed much to the unformulated

English Constitution which, interestingly enough, they knew best from Montesquieu's misinterpretation of it. Hamilton in organizing treasury administration leaned upon British fiscal experience, and there is very direct connection between the Bank of England and the first Bank of the United States. In the conduct of foreign affairs and in the organization and administration of the tiny war machine there are probably similar relationships. There is an active interest now at work in the United States in administrative history, and those most concerned would profit by knowledge of related British experience.

When the frame of government of the New Republic had been completed there began a troubled relationship with the various European governments which has been very extensively studied, particularly its Anglo-American phase. Scholars on both sides of the Atlantic have long been interested in the way in which long-standing enemies and rivals became allies. So we may now be more profitably concerned with the internal development of the United States. This invites study in comparison with that of Britain in phases which are less obvious.

Population movement, population assimilation, organizing new communities were important experiences in both societies. In the United States there was a western movement of population; likewise, the progress of the industrial revolution was tending to concentrate a larger proportion of the population in towns. These shifts in population brought the need of readjusting political institutions. In the western country new political units, such as territories and states, were in constant process of creation, while in the older regions, city governments had to be organized to take care of the boroughs and towns that had outgrown the simpler forms. These processes expanded the franchise.

Greater attention began to be paid to the locus of power. Originally the central government had little; indeed, during the period of the unfortunate War of 1812, the central government was almost abandoned by the people. But the great growth of the nation presented the possibility of government subsidy, and those who gained power and controlled government would decide who was to get what. Political power brought greater rewards and they were more fiercely striven for. These potentialities made politics more intense, the politicians more competitive and the newly enfranchised voters were more ardently bombarded with importunity. A ruthlessness was added to political dynamics.

Here in England in the same period, 1815–60, there

were trends of a similar character. Population was flowing out to the colonies or crowding into the new industrial cities. English political talent was busy with creating new societies and governments in Canada and Australia and wrestling with problems of group antagonism and racial and religious conflict in India. Agitation for a reform in the suffrage was parallel with the growth of democracy in the United States, and the repeal of the Corn Laws was almost coincident in date with the Walker tariff across the sea, which was the culmination of a thirty-year struggle ending in a compromise which did not deal too unkindly with the budding industries.

The effort to organize an effective federal system in the United States harmonizing the interests of semi-independent states with a growing nationalism parallels somewhat the evolution going on within the empire. Fortunately, Britain escaped the tragedy of a civil war such as the United States suffered, but difficulties in India, Ireland and South Africa put strains on the evolving democracy. The United States emerged from the Civil War with a revised federal system. Central power was stronger, but local power was by no means destroyed. Slow steps were taken in the direction of regional administrative units like the Federal Reserve Bank Districts. By another evolutionary process, the British devised the type of federalism known as the Commonwealth of Nations.

A further step in the history of the Anglo-American democratic experience was the definition of the relation of government to public weal. The development of urbanization, mechanized industry and improvements in all types of communication, which ultimately seem to have annihilated certain concepts of time and space, have made many adjustments necessary in human relations. Would ancient patterns of governmental action fit new conditions of society? In both the United States and Britain these changes affected democratic behaviour significantly, and the process invites comparison and cross-study by scholars on both sides of the Atlantic. In both societies there has been a shift from the *laisser-faire* philosophy of the early nineteenth century to what has become Labour government in Britain and the New Deal in the United States. The exhilarating air breathed by the apostles of free industrial enterprise proved too stimulating. The American society found capitalists and corporations possessed of power which was being abused to the detriment of society, and doctrines of social control had to be formulated and new functions added to those assigned to government by the Constitution. The political technique of thus altering the government has had its British counterpart; they may be described as another element in the common experience.

Latterly, there has been the shared realization of the world responsibility of the democracies which has brought such new stresses and strains upon the machinery of democracy. Among these the administration of colonies, hemisphere defence, war-making and the combating of subversive philosophies and underground political activities have been but a few. The charge that democracy could not meet these tests has been refuted.

IV. *Possible Methods of Co-operative Study of Democratic Behaviour*

Thus I have outlined some of the possibilities of the study of Anglo-American experience by representatives of the two cultures. Each of the occupants of this chair will undoubtedly be thinking in some relationship to this joint experience. You here will be able to gather the varying points of view into your own assembly of ideas.

My own particular interest in this study of Anglo-American experience is in the mechanism of political action. Despite the fact that so much attention has been devoted to political and constitutional history, too little thought has been given to the evolution of the basic patterns of political behaviour.

Judging by political history in the United States there is no adequate analysis of the evolution of the real instruments of democratic behaviour, namely, the parties. There is much in the way of political biography but in concentrating on the leaders, little or no attention has been paid to the led. It is knowledge of the political behaviour of the mass, and the reasons therefore, not of the few in positions of party leadership or in legislative position, that we need.

We need fresh study of the two–party system, that achievement almost unique of the Anglo-American endeavour. It is the chief mechanism of democracy, but unfortunately the practical working of this system has been much distorted in historical writing. Political historians have been more interested in personalities, in the artificial dialectic of political debate and in certain spectacular political events than they have been concerned with the history of actual political behaviour and operation. In place of exclusive interest in prominent leaders, so-called political issues and the incidents and statistics of campaigning, we now seek the more intricate causes of mass political behaviour. Instead of so much emphasis upon what might be called the formal and visible history of government as operated by party in executive and legislative functioning, we seek the less visible, in fact often hidden, operation of party machinery in matters of patronage, of designation of candidates for office, of party funds and of the activities of these most potent party managers who never hold office. I understand that in Britain you do not have as much political machinery as we do, and you have given even less historical attention to it than we have.

The basis of party politics is an understanding, instinctive or rationalized, of popular attitudes. Political leaders, greater and lesser, must place themselves in effective relationship with those attitudes either in forming, altering or following them. The crux of the historian's problem is to understand the evolution of this relationship between those in politics and these public attitudes. It is no narrow concept, for it means the political historian must be a widely read student of 'Kulturgeschichte' and work its main themes into any analogies he may make.

It is now more apparent than it ever has been before that the technique necessary is that involved in the study of cultural history. Politics is but part of a composite pattern of the behaviour of society, and it is closely related to many other forms of behaviour. Consequently, it is essential to be actively interested in social analysis and to secure from the work of those in the other social sciences their ideas and methods. Two are of primary concern, the knowledge of social attitudes and their formation and adjustment, and the capturing and measure of public opinion. Much progress has been made by psychologists and political scientists in these forms of analysis, but too little of this interest or technique has been much utilized by historians. The result has been contentment with too naïve and simple explanations of political thought and action.

An example of this simplicity which has been the cause of much historical inadequacy can be cited from the pages of the history of the United States. It has been the custom to study American political history as though it were mainly concerned with the growth of two national parties. But this is only part of the story and perhaps not the more important part. Our parties have in reality seldom been really national, for central party management has never truly been achieved except at rare intervals. We, in fact, should have been studying a series of state parties, for in the United States each state maintains a separate and quite autonomous party system, and these state parties act with great independence. While their leaders co-operate periodically in national elections, and sometimes in Congress, they always maintain much of this autonomy.

Political behaviour, in fact, is conditioned primarily by the situations in the localities in which the voters reside. When interest exists in so-called national issues these national situations must still be studied, but so much of the electoral interest is local, so many fundamental political attitudes are formed by local situations, that it is essential to pay much more attention to the machinery of local political operation. To find what are the real influences moulding political action, it is necessary to know local group tensions, prejudices, enthusiasms. It is likewise necessary to study leadership at its roots, namely, in the relations of local leaders and followers.

The examination of local units shows a variety of attitudes, some of them common to many localities, others uniquely situated. Close examination of these attitudes and their distribution sometimes makes it necessary to revise long-held simplifications. In the study of the political antecedents of the American Civil War, the fact that the conflict itself finally took place between two societies located in separate regions made it easy to conclude that sectionalism or regionalism upon which were based two antagonistic societies was the simple cause. Two powers, it was easy to say, were struggling for control of the federal system. However, an examination of the significant attitudes shaping political behaviour revealed not two, northern and southern, but at least ten basic attitudes. Some of these, like anti-slavery opinion, southernism, New Englandism, territorialism and metropolitanism, were in conflict with others which were designed to bring harmony, and the conflict was intensified because of the religious and romantic attitudes which were shared by all and made for intensity of emotion and for a woeful lack of realism. The problem then which the political leaders faced, failed to understand, and were unable to solve, was not how to keep the balance of power in a political federalism. Rather it was how to keep this variety of attitudes which were not localized but found everywhere in some kind of a balanced cultural federal system. This cultural federal system was one in which the attitudes were units, just as states were the units in the political federal system.

Likewise, a post-Civil War situation demands more intensive analysis. The disaster of the Civil War seems to have taught political leaders a lesson which they instinctively rather than consciously assimilated and which needs further study. Ordinarily, we think of the latter part of the nineteenth century as a period in which American political activity was mainly involved

in working out means of developing new governmental functions of social control in a fashion truly
democratic and progressive, that is, in the Whig
tradition. But there was something else developing
which needs more study. The increasing population
and the larger number of states, together with the
tendency toward a great inequality in the distribution
of the national income, meant that the variety of
attitudes and the danger of their intense conflict were
increasing.

In order to avoid civil disorder the political leaders,
I feel sure instinctively rather than consciously, began
to reorganize the two great parties into institutions
which would not fight on significant issues, that would
be so much in agreement on basic principles that any
change in power would in no significant way alter the
general character of government. Membership in the
parties became a matter of custom, inheritance or local
condition. Burning questions were avoided, and the
partisanship was institutionalized so as to be as
socially innocuous as possible. Partisanship and
political activity took on the characteristics of sport
which thrilled and entertained people. Politics was
likewise akin to religion; people 'believed in' the
Republican party and were loyal to it because socially
it was the thing to do. One was born into a family,

a nation, a religion and a party and was loyal to all. A mythology of party history was accepted. The nature of this process needs more study, for this cohesive power of democracy needs to be cultivated in this world of ours.

These are some of the problems of the evolution of political democracy which are in process of study in America and upon which we need the counsel of British scholars. Here in Britain there is much to be learned. In particular, here should be found the secret of why Anglo-Americans have been so successful in maintaining a two-party system and avoiding the tendency to 'Splitterpartei' that so affects significant parts of continental Europe. We may further consider the hypothesis that it arises out of the experiences of Britain between 55 B.C. and A.D. 1066, when the island was invaded by Romans, Angles and Saxons, Danes and Normans. During this millennium there was a succession of two-party situations in which the parties were the conquered and the conquerors. It became a continuous social condition to have two groups often well-defined in opposition. The inhabitants of this island learned to make this adjustment, and if I read history aright the Normans, at least, cleverly worked at this adjustment as they created their administrative system.

Americans, students of politics, can profit also from further study of English experience in the fifteenth and seventeenth centuries. The contests between the White Rose and the Red, between Roundhead and Cavalier, may throw light on American political origin. So will more knowledge of the political habits of the average Englishman in the Tudor century, for it was those habits which the founders of the thirteen colonies brought to America. Also Irish experience will be helpful, because so many emigrants from Little Britain came to America when our political parties were forming. They immediately proved adept at politics, and as Brogan has suggested to me, they showed this proficiency because of their home customs of political activity.

If then this joint Anglo-American experience is submitted to the examination of scholars on both sides of the Atlantic with frequent exchange of views and findings, much will be learned. This will be particularly true if we approach the problem with certain of the categories of modern social analysis in mind: if we use the findings of the behaviouristic and social psychologists in motivation and in group psychology; if we consider rather judiciously some of the techniques of psychiatry; if we utilize what the demographers tell us of the behaviour of population in relation to physiographic environment, particularly the influence of soil in conditioning ways of living; if we study the relation of business and emotional cycles of behaviour to the cycles of political behaviour marked by the rise and fall of ruling parties or interests. If we follow these paths much will be accomplished to make the study of political behaviour in democracy more realistic and more meaningful.

Closely allied with this opportunity is another responsibility, the responsibility for seeing that adequate contemporary records are made. Those active in the practical side of politics, those who bear much of the burden and heat of the day are notoriously bad at keeping records. Occasionally one such keeps a diary, or his correspondence, but nowadays when the automobile, the aeroplane and the telephone are used, so much is never recorded. Parties, if our American organizations are examples, have no system of record keeping which is of much use to the historian. Therefore it is essential that scholars make much more serious effort to find out how things are happening at the time and make the record. They may be almost certain that it will not be made for them.

Thus we have considered some of the many potentialities of this chair. Each year new ideas and varying points of view should be brought here. However, you may conclude that it would be well to conserve some cumulative result from these visits. Cambridge historians are noted for their co-operative endeavours. Could not some Cambridge scholar act as co-operator with the successive American visitors? He could work with those who come here on a new series in the notable Cambridge Histories, each to be responsible for a particular section or series of chapters. There might emerge a 'Cambridge History of Democracy'.

V. *The Larger Implications of Anglo-American Historical Co-operation*

Fresh study of the democratic experience can be one of great significance. Both Britain and the United States are experiencing a number of vital changes in democratic procedures. The policies of the Labour government here and the New Deal in the United States have been evidences of changing patterns of democracy. But these changes in democracy are not sufficiently understood. Many prate of democracy who are thinking in terms of the Victorian Age or in America looking back to the days of William McKinley. In fact, in any epoch of confusion, people turn to history, pick out other days that seem more fortunate, and sigh for those golden ages. This sort of nostalgia, this thinking of democracy in terms which no longer are valid, is bound to be confusing and may be dangerous.

In further research into the workings of Anglo-American democracy we should seek the truth not blinded by nationalistic thinking, or by Whig-Progressive traditions. Neither should the historian allow his prevailing mood of optimism or more likely pessimism to colour his thinking. This brief comparison which I have been making indicates the background for my belief that there are so many common elements in the Anglo-American experience that in a very real sense they should not be considered, as they generally now are, as independent developments, nor by the historians of each society working independently.

Strong as are our patriotic impulses, and highly as we value love and loyalty to native land, nevertheless, as historians we must realize that nationalism is a barrier to historical understanding. All during the nineteenth century, when history took such impressive strides ahead, the historians were working in an atmosphere heavy with rising nationalism. Almost unconsciously the histories of the various states took on that colouring, and that colouring emphasized separateness and uniqueness. Rivalries and jealousies were reflected consciously or unconsciously, and too often those in one society thought of others only as aliens who, like their language, must be understood in a different medium of thought, expression and interpretation—with little concept of anything common or kindred. As I have indicated above American historians have been much the slaves of this nationalism.

Also, particularly in these two democracies, there has been such great weight given to a particular colour of political influence and tradition in a fashion which may at times partially obscure the truth. In Great Britain and in the United States it is a commonplace, for those who give any heed to these things, to consider the trend of national development generally in terms of righteous striving with a great degree of success toward moral and social progress. This produces in Great Britain the Whig tradition which, as I have indicated, is matched by the people's or the progressive tradition in the United States. Thus historians in these two societies are almost constantly operating with beams in their eyes, sometimes conscious of motes in the eyes of their contemporaries elsewhere, but almost never aware of the hindrance to their own sight.

Therefore I believe that truth in history demands a conscious effort to consider the narrowing effect of employing such interpretive concepts as are supplied by nationalism and Whiggery when used too exclusively in studying democracy and to discover more comprehensive interpretations. This may well be attempted by the occupants of this chair as they sojourn with you periodically, but it can best be accomplished, I believe, if some plan is worked out for co-operative study.

Finally, in so doing it is well to assume a more realistic philosophy of history. We do not stand at any point of climax or calamity or at any peak or depression. We happen to stand somewhere in the midst of continuing experience—much has preceded—much will follow. There is no reason to assume that what has gone before is better—so cannot be used as escape—nor inferior—so that we can look ahead with blinding optimism. Nor should we look ahead to millennium or catastrophe—but to more of the same. What is this same for which historians should look? The objects of study should be the universal patterns of experience sought without manic hysteria or melancholia, without fear or elation. We study not rise nor fall so much as change, constant, ceaseless change, and change which in a sense is seldom very basic. Basically, that is, organically, physiologically, man is still equipped just as he was when he first appeared with the characteristics of *Homo sapiens*. The great mystery now, as always, is: What are the limits of his brain capacity?

Thus the growing interest in the study of American history in a British University, of which the inauguration of this chair is such encouraging evidence, is an invitation for a union of the scholars of democracy to work together. While thus co-operating it is essential that they reappraise their methodology and seek the best techniques to enable them to correct dispassionately the deviations in the path toward truth caused by the strength of their emotions and their traditions.

From the past we learn the lesson of the great planning skill and ambitious intelligence of Anglo-American enterprise. It has created states and empires, socially enlightened commonwealths and mature cultures. Surely in these times, if ever, this genius should be invoked for the salvaging of western civilization. There is no reason to believe that this great creative capacity is exhausted. May the cultural co-operation which the establishing of this chair represents bear fruit in significant contributions from the association of American visitors with the Cambridge fellowship.

www.ingramcontent.com/pod-product-compliance
Ingram Content Group UK Ltd.
Pitfield, Milton Keynes, MK11 3LW, UK
UKHW020448010325
455719UK00015B/484